anced

PL IS

Specific Skill Series
for Language Arts

Vocabulary

Leveled Books in Nine Key Language Arts Skill Areas

Columbus, OH

The McGraw-Hill Companies

Cover: ©PhotoDisc/Getty Images, Inc.

SRAonline.com

McGraw Hill SRA

Send all inquiries to:
SRA/McGraw-Hill
8787 Orion Place
Columbus, OH 43240-4027

Printed in the United States of America.

ISBN 0-07-601741-9

2 3 4 5 6 7 8 9 RHR 14 13 12 11 10

TO THE TEACHER

ABOUT THE *PLACEMENT TESTS*

Teachers can use the *Placement Tests* for each skill area to determine how to place students in the appropriate level of the program. There are three test levels: Primary, Intermediate, and Advanced. Each test level includes two forms of tests—Form X and Form Y. Either form may be used as a pretest for student placement or a posttest to measure student progress. The following chart can be used as a guide for determining which test level to administer to each student.

Test Level	Appropriate for Students at Level. . .
Primary	A, B, or C (Grades 1-3)
Intermediate	D, E, or F (Grades 4-6)
Advanced	G or H (Grades 7-8)

Primary and Intermediate tests are each twelve pages long, and Advanced tests are eight pages long to allow for accurate assessment of students' skill levels. The tests consist of representative pages selected from the Student Editions; four pages are selected from each level, as shown on the chart below. Teachers may, if they wish, administer only four pages of a test at a time to determine if a student should advance to the next level.

Test Level	Page Numbers	Selected from Level. . .	Test Level	Page Numbers	Selected from Level. . .
Primary Form X	6-9	A	Primary Form Y	40-43	A
	10-13	B		44-47	B
	14-17	C		48-51	C
Intermediate Form X	18-21	D	Intermediate Form Y	52-55	D
	22-25	E		56-59	E
	26-29	F		60-63	F
Advanced Form X	30-33	G	Advanced Form Y	64-67	G
	34-37	H		68-71	H

INSTRUCTIONS FOR USING THE *PLACEMENT TESTS*

1. Students should be instructed to turn to the page corresponding to the level and form of the test that is to be administered. The tests are not designed to be timed, but teachers may choose to set a time limit for the completion of a test.
2. Students should record their answers on the worksheet found in the back of this book or on separate pieces of paper. No answer should be recorded in the *Placement Test* books.
3. Check students' answers using the Answer Keys in the *Teacher's Manual,* and use the scale below as a guide for placement if administering the entire test.

Test Level	Score	Placement Level
Primary	lower than 40%	A
	40%-79%	B
	80% or higher	C (or D if score is 98% or higher)
Intermediate	lower than 40%	D
	40%-79%	E
	80% or higher	F (or G if score is 98% or higher)
Advanced	lower than 75%	G
	75% or higher	H

TABLE OF CONTENTS
PLACEMENT TESTS FORM X

Specific Skill Series
for Language Arts

Vocabulary

PLACEMENT TESTS

FORM X

Primary
Intermediate
Advanced

Which word does *not* fit each category?

1. Feelings

(A) glad

(B) proud

(C) smell

2. Things That Are Heavy

(A) rock

(B) leaf

(C) log

3. Jobs

(A) nurse

(B) judge

(C) beach

4. Parts of Your Face

(A) knees

(B) nose

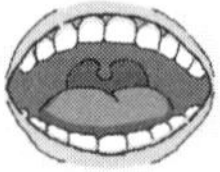
(C) mouth

Match each word to its synonym.

5. talk  **(A)** tale

6. shut  **(B)** skip

7. story  **(C)** speak

8. hop  **(D)** giggle

9. house  **(E)** close

10. laugh 

(F) home

Match each word on the left to its homograph on the right.

11. fan

12. hood

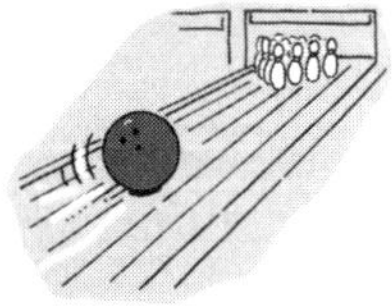

13. bowl

14. fly

15. pitcher

(A) a person who likes something a lot

(B) a deep dish

(C) to move in the air with wings

(D) a baseball player

(E) part of a coat

Choose a word from the box to make a compound word that describes each picture.

(A) guard	**(B)** after	**(C)** note	**(D)** pack

16. back____

17. ____book

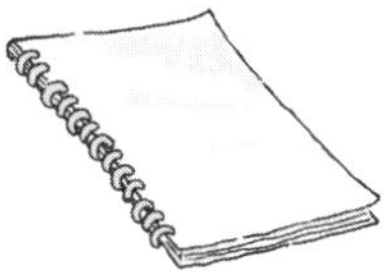

18. life____

19. ____noon

Which word pairs are synonyms?

20. (A) goal—purpose **(B)** goal—life

21. (A) page—sheet **(B)** page—chapter

22. (A) child—adult **(B)** child—youth

23. (A) form—share **(B)** form—shape

24. (A) pile—stack **(B)** pile—watch

25. (A) pair—apple **(B)** pair—two

26. (A) rude—nice **(B)** rude—thoughtless

27. (A) load—weight **(B)** load—pen

28. (A) lawn—tree **(B)** lawn—grass

What is the antonym for the underlined word in each sentence?

29. <u>Remember</u> to brush your teeth after every meal.
(A) forget
(B) understand

---

30. A pair of cardinals will stay <u>together</u> for life.
(A) apart
(B) connected

---

31. It is <u>common</u> for young children to take naps.
(A) rare
(B) bad

---

32. Fog is a cloud of <u>moist</u> air.
(A) soft
(B) dry

---

33. Storage bins will help keep your room <u>tidy</u>.
(A) large
(B) messy

---

34. A rumor is something a person hears from someone else that may or may not be <u>true</u>.
(A) pretty
(B) false

Choose the base word of the underlined word in each sentence.

35. My baby brother is allowed to play with unbreakable toys only.
(A) break
(B) breaking

---

36. Lydia went to art school to become a designer.
(A) design
(B) redesign

---

37. The overripe banana attracted fruit flies.
(A) ripeness
(B) ripe

---

38. Kenji dislocated his elbow while playing on the jungle gym.
(A) locate
(B) dislocate

---

39. It is undeniable that George Washington was the first president of the United States.
(A) denied
(B) deny

Choose the definition of the underlined word in each context. Look for contrast clues.

40. Gavin thought he would be <u>nervous</u> before his performance. To his surprise, he was calm.
(A) fearful and jumpy
(B) surprised

---

41. In the wild, adult tigers are not very <u>social</u>. They like to live alone.
(A) hungry
(B) friendly

---

42. Instead of being unkind, the <u>merciful</u> man forgave his enemy.
(A) showing kindness
(B) feeling sick

---

43. The <u>exterior</u> of the car was white, but the inside was covered in black leather.
(A) outside
(B) roof

Choose the synonym for the underlined word in each sentence.

44. Children continue their <u>education</u> in the fall after summer vacation.
(A) schooling **(B)** fitness **(C)** theater

45. The leaves of a maple tree turn red in <u>autumn</u>.
(A) summer **(B)** fall **(C)** season

46. My dog and I like to <u>leap</u> onto the piles of leaves.
(A) fall **(B)** walk **(C)** jump

47. Sometimes you can smell leaves <u>burning</u> in the evening air.
(A) falling **(B)** blazing **(C)** curling

48. The <u>chilly</u> air smells fresh during evening walks.
(A) hot **(B)** warm **(C)** cold

49. We <u>store</u> our summer clothes in the basement.
(A) put away **(B)** mall **(C)** pass

50. The squirrels and other animals <u>collect</u> food for the winter.
(A) scatter **(B)** gather **(C)** eat

51. Fall is the season for <u>jackets</u> and football.
(A) coats **(B)** scarves **(C)** gloves

Read each sentence. Then choose the idiom that best matches the meaning of the underlined words.

52. Please watch for the arrival of the school bus.
(A) keep an eye out
(B) have eyes in the back of your head

53. If you eat large amounts of food, you might gain weight.
(A) eat one's words
(B) eat like a horse

54. If someone is rude, you must often accept and put up with it.
(A) go off the deep end
(B) grin and bear it

55. When the cat knocked over a lamp, I was surprised and shocked.
(A) jumped out of my skin
(B) jumped the track

56. Sue forgot and told me about the surprise party.
(A) let the cat out of the bag
(B) let the chance slip by

57. The class was listening very closely during the important announcement.
(A) all ears
(B) out of hand

Use the clues in each sentence to choose the prefix that belongs in the blank.

58. The explorers ____covered the buried treasure.
(A) bi- **(B)** mis- **(C)** un-

---

59. You should ____check a letter for errors after reading it the first time.
(A) un- **(B)** re- **(C)** pre-

---

60. Nobody should ever ____treat an animal.
(A) mis- **(B)** un- **(C)** re-

---

61. If you write in a journal two times every week, you write in it ____weekly.
(A) pre- **(B)** mis- **(C)** bi-

---

62. When you see part of a movie before it is officially released, you are seeing a ____view.
(A) im- **(B)** pre- **(C)** re-

---

63. Something that is not perfect is ____perfect.
(A) im- **(B)** bi- **(C)** mis-

---

64. Somebody who is not mature is ____mature.
(A) im- **(B)** bi- **(C)** pre-

---

65. A ____cycle has two wheels.
(A) mis- **(B)** bi- **(C)** pre-

Choose the definition of the underlined word in each context. Look for contrast clues.

66. A cat has <u>retractable</u> claws, but a dog's claws are always out.
(A) sharp
(B) able to be pulled in

67. Instead of being selfish, the <u>charitable</u> group volunteered almost all their free time to clean the park.
(A) being generous
(B) feeling happy

68. Reptiles as pets are usually <u>distant</u>. They are not as loving as some mammals.
(A) not needing affection
(B) quiet

69. May and June <u>precede</u> July; however, November comes after it.
(A) go along with
(B) come before

70. Most of the people in the crowd brought jackets, but only a <u>handful</u> had umbrellas.
(A) a small amount
(B) a particular person

PRIMARY—FORM X ends on this page.

That's Bizarre!

Choose the homophone that completes each sentence.

1. In ancient Greece, people voted by scratching a candidate's name inside the shell of a _____.
(A) mussel **(B)** muscle

2. _____, or corn, is an ingredient used to make chewing gum.
(A) Maize **(B)** Maze

3. A chameleon's skin color can _____ depending on its mood.
(A) very **(B)** vary

4. It is possible for a _____ to jump 150 times its own length.
(A) flea **(B)** flee

5. There are several different types of _____ in the ocean that look like the human brain.
(A) coral **(B)** choral

6. A museum in Wépion, Belgium, is devoted solely to the straw_____.
(A) bury **(B)** berry

7. The skunk cabbage is a plant that has the _____ of a skunk.
(A) cent **(B)** scent

8. Spending time in a _____ room can make your pulse rate slow down and your body temperature drop.
(A) blue **(B)** blew

9. A cow _____ its food twice; the second time, the food is called "cud."
(A) choose **(B)** chews

10. Carbon dioxide-emitting bacteria cause bubbles that make Swiss cheese _____.
(A) holey **(B)** wholly

Are the words in each word pair synonyms or antonyms?

11. complete—begin
(A) synonyms **(B)** antonyms

12. enthusiastic—thrilled
(A) synonyms **(B)** antonyms

13. ask—inquire
(A) synonyms **(B)** antonyms

14. give—receive
(A) synonyms **(B)** antonyms

15. successful—prosperous
(A) synonyms **(B)** antonyms

16. tranquil—calm
(A) synonyms **(B)** antonyms

Which word pair completes each analogy?

17. *Complete* is to *begin* as . . .
(A) *center* is to *middle.* **(B)** *inside* is to *outside.*

18. *Enthusiastic* is to *thrilled* as . . .
(A) *shame* is to *embarrassment.* **(B)** *shame* is to *cry.*

19. *Ask* is to *inquire* as . . .
(A) *prevail* is to *win.* **(B)** *mellow* is to *nervous.*

20. *Give* is to *receive* as . . .
(A) *develop* is to *grow.* **(B)** *stop* is to *start.*

21. *Successful* is to *prosperous* as . . .
(A) *dispute* is to *argue.* **(B)** *dispute* is to *agree.*

22. *Tranquil* is to *calm* as . . .
(A) *obedient* is to *dutiful.* **(B)** *exposed* is to *hidden.*

Choose the Latin or Greek root to correctly complete each word.

23. A _____graphy is a person's life story written by someone else.
(A) photo
(B) bio

---

24. _____marine is a bluish-green color that resembles ocean water.
(A) Bio
(B) Aqua

---

25. An employer cannot re_____ an application for employment based on the applicant's age, gender, or race.
(A) ject
(B) photo

---

26. An im_____ is a product that has been brought into a country from another country.
(A) bio
(B) port

---

27. _____graphy is the art and science of using light to produce images on sensitive surfaces, such as film.
(A) Photo
(B) Cyclo

---

28. The four seasons are _____ical because they follow the same pattern each year.
(A) cycl
(B) ject

---

29. Plants _____synthesize, or create carbohydrates in their leaves, when they are exposed to light.
(A) photo
(B) bio

Read each dictionary entry. Choose the number of the definition that fits the meaning of the underlined word in each sentence.

slip (slip) *verb.* **1.** to lose one's balance or footing; slide suddenly or accidentally: *to slip on icy steps.* **2.** to pass unnoticed: *Another month slipped by.* **3.** to make a mistake: *I slipped on the test's last question.*

30. "I don't know how your birthday slipped by me," Carol said.
(A) 1 **(B)** 2 **(C)** 3

---

31. The gymnast slipped off the balance beam, but she still won the competition.
(A) 1 **(B)** 2 **(C)** 3

---

32. The news reporter slipped by saying "Revolutionary War" when he meant to say "Civil War."
(A) 1 **(B)** 2 **(C)** 3

post (pōst) *noun.* **1.** an upright piece of wood, stone, or other solid material, usually used as a support or marker. **2.** a place where a soldier, police officer, or the like is stationed or assigned for duty: *assigned to a post.* **3.** a system by which mail is collected, carried, and delivered.

33. A fence needs several posts to anchor it to the ground.
(A) 1 **(B)** 2 **(C)** 3

---

34. From April 1860 to October 1861, people who lived in the western United States could use the Pony Express to send letters by post.
(A) 1 **(B)** 2 **(C)** 3

---

35. The guards were ordered not to leave their posts except in an emergency.
(A) 1 **(B)** 2 **(C)** 3

Choose an ANTONYM for the underlined word in each sentence.

36. The covered wagon was the most common way for families to travel to Montana.
(A) usual (B) unusual (C) expert (D) inland

37. "Prairie schooners" were converted farm wagons used by the majority of travelers of the time.
(A) desired (B) minority (C) brevity (D) complexity

38. There was room in the wagons for only the most fundamental supplies.
(A) boring (B) attractive (C) basic (D) unnecessary

39. Because of the discomfort of wagon travel, many people walked beside the wagon.
(A) difficulties (B) ease (C) disgust (D) effectiveness

40. Families crossing the vast country often encountered many hardships.
(A) avoided (B) suffered (C) grasped (D) met

41. Travelers learned that hundreds of other settlers were experiencing identical conditions.
(A) similar (B) terrifying (C) different (D) defeated

42. The desire to own land was one of the main reasons a pioneer spirit existed in the nineteenth century.
(A) lurked (B) entered (C) chased (D) vanished

43. The promise of vast, open landscapes, abundant wildlife, and unspoiled rivers and lakes fueled settlers' hopes and dreams.
(A) polluted (B) fantastic (C) small (D) clear

INTERMEDIATE—FORM X

Choose the pair of words that best completes each analogy. Each analogy will compare synonyms *or* antonyms.

44. *Elder* is to *younger* as _____.
(A) *sudden* is to *gradual* **(B)** *brave* is to *bold*

45. *Elaborate* is to *detailed* as _____.
(A) *brilliant* is to *glittering* **(B)** *tedious* is to *exciting*

46. *Prick* is to *pierce* as _____.
(A) *sweltering* is to *chilly* **(B)** *cram* is to *stuff*

47. *Jeer* is to *praise* as _____.
(A) *destroy* is to *ruin* **(B)** *unite* is to *divide*

48. *Inferior* is to *lesser* as _____.
(A) *vague* is to *uncertain* **(B)** *remote* is to *near*

49. *Primary* is to *secondary* as _____.
(A) *transfer* is to *move* **(B)** *permanent* is to *temporary*

50. *Numeral* is to *number* as _____.

(A) *pantry* is to *food* **(B)** *novice* is to *beginner*

51. *Utter* is to *speak* as _____.
(A) *begin* is to *conclude* **(B)** *hunch* is to *guess*

52. *Outlook* is to *viewpoint* as _____.
(A) *atrocious* is to *lovely* **(B)** *bellow* is to *roar*

53. *Improve* is to *worsen* as _____.
(A) *pure* is to *contaminated* **(B)** *nuisance* is to *pest*

54. *Foe* is to *enemy* as _____.
(A) *cunning* is to *clever* **(B)** *public* is to *private*

Choose the Latin or Greek root to correctly complete each word.

55. We didn't understand how the chemical process worked, so we asked our teacher for _____ification.
(A) log
(B) clar

---

56. Advertisers study the _____graphics of a television show, including the average age of the viewers, before they decide to sponsor it.
(A) demo
(B) phil

---

57. Meteorologists are able to pre_____, or foretell, what the weather will be for a couple days in advance.
(A) dict
(B) log

---

58. The _____orium was filled with students, all eager to hear what the governor had to say.
(A) clar
(B) audit

---

59. _____*adelphia* means "city of brotherly love."
(A) *Phil*
(B) *Clar*

---

60. The early _____cratic party in the United States believed that the people, rather than the federal government, should have the most power.
(A) Demo
(B) Audit

---

61. A dia_____ue is a conversation between two or more people.
(A) clar
(B) log

Read each paragraph, and look for comparison or contrast clues. Use those clues to answer the questions.

Some changes in American life over the last hundred years have been slight, but changes in transportation have been truly significant. For example, the first trains were seen at the time as being incredibly rapid, but modern airplanes are so fast that a trip on one of those trains today would seem quite sluggish. Still, the people who packed their valises (much like today's suitcases, but without wheels) in 1832 got just as homesick on long trips as we do.

62. What is the definition of *sluggish?*
(A) useless or hopeless
(B) having little motion, speed, or activity

---

63. What is the definition of *valise?*
(A) a small piece of luggage
(B) a person who collects tickets or fares

The ancestors of today's dogs were wild creatures, unlike the domesticated animals we now have as pets. At first, dogs and humans were enemies. However, early dogs were predators, and humans were also hunters. Humans were better at it, and dogs soon learned that it was practical to live with people, where there was usually food. Dogs became accepted because they could help in the hunt and guard campsites and homes. The relationship between dogs and people became an example of symbiosis, like the relationship between bees and flowers in which each helps the other.

64. What is the definition of *domesticated?*
(A) living with and near people and cared for by them
(B) of or belonging to the period before recorded history

---

65. What is the definition of *predator?*
(A) one who can be attacked or is not protected
(B) an animal that lives by preying on other animals

---

66. What is the definition of *symbiosis?*
(A) the inability to change to deal with new conditions
(B) a helpful relationship between living beings that are not alike

Native Americans and the United States Government

Choose the definition for the homograph underlined in each sentence.

67. Native Americans had a contract with the government called a *treaty.*
(A) a binding agreement **(B)** to become smaller

____

68. Hundreds of years ago, Native Americans were content to live off the land.
(A) satisfied **(B)** subject matter of a written work

____

69. In 1815 the Iroquois were limited to reservations near the town of Buffalo, New York.
(A) limited conditions **(B)** tracts of public land set aside

____

70. Legislation passed in 1819 provided government money to train Native Americans in agriculture.
(A) a series of railroad cars **(B)** to teach so as to make qualified

____

71. President Andrew Jackson drove Native Americans from their lands in the 1830s.
(A) forced out **(B)** to transport in a vehicle

____

72. The tribes were sent to land that was not good for growing crops.
(A) cuts off **(B)** produce of cultivated plants

____

73. Some tribes refused to trade their land and were forced to march westward.
(A) exchange or barter **(B)** a business of a certain nature

____

74. The legislation that was passed reversed the previous policy of respecting the rights of Native Americans.
(A) revoked or overruled **(B)** turned inside out

Choose the pair of words that best completes each analogy.

75. *Tension* is to *stress* as _____.
(A) *victory* is to *defeat* (B) *surrender* is to *concede*

76. *Abbreviate* is to *lengthen* as _____.
(A) *restrict* is to *expand* (B) *retrieve* is to *capture*

77. *Superior* is to *subordinate* as _____.
(A) *wealth* is to *poverty* (B) *proud* is to *arrogant*

78. *Ghastly* is to *frightful* as _____.
(A) *intense* is to *sluggish* (B) *exclusive* is to *unique*

79. *Patriot* is to *nationalist* as _____.
(A) *selfish* is to *generous* (B) *payment* is to *compensation*

80. *Alert* is to *drowsy* as _____.
(A) *ludicrous* is to *absurd* (B) *unbelievable* is to *credible*

81. *Vanquish* is to *subdue* as _____.
(A) *explain* is to *confuse* (B) *demonstrate* is to *illustrate*

82. *Remember* is to *recollect* as _____.
(A) *imprisonment* is to *incarceration* (B) *glance* is to *stare*

83. *Laughter* is to *mirth* as _____.
(A) *fearful* is to *intrepid* (B) *judgment* is to *verdict*

84. *Joy* is to *ecstasy* as _____.
(A) *casual* is to *nonchalant* (B) *advance* is to *retreat*

85. *Gather* is to *disperse* as _____.
(A) *curious* is to *inquisitive* (B) *orderly* is to *chaotic*

86. *Educated* is to *illiterate* as _____.
(A) *critical* is to *praising* (B) *scholarly* is to *learned*

87. *Arrival* is to *departure* as _____.
(A) *simple* is to *complex* (B) *exceed* is to *surpass*

Charles Marion Russell

Use the clues in each sentence to choose the prefix that belongs in the blank.

88. Charles Russell's _____taste for studying led him to leave school and become a cowboy in Montana at the age of sixteen.
(A) dis- **(B)** tri- **(C)** multi-

---

89. When he later decided to dedicate his time to painting, his parents were _____assured by the fact that he was already a talented artist.
(A) ir- **(B)** dis- **(C)** re-

---

90. The hunting tales told by his Native American friends in Montana and Canada were of _____estimable value to him because they provided ideas for much of his work.
(A) re- **(B)** dis- **(C)** in-

---

91. He considered the _____appearance of the bison a symbol of the death of the Old West.
(A) tri- **(B)** multi- **(C)** dis-

---

92. He saw their eradication as an _____recoverable loss.
(A) ir- **(B)** re- **(C)** tri-

---

93. His detailed paintings of the _____angular shape of tepees serve as historical records of the structure of Native American dwellings.
(A) multi- **(B)** dis- **(C)** tri-

---

94. The artist's _____colored paintings with their dramatic lighting leave a lasting impression on the viewer.
(A) un- **(B)** in- **(C)** multi-

Choose the Latin or Greek root to correctly complete each word.

95. Keesha chattered _____atedly about her first day at school.
(A) neo
(B) pan
(C) anim

---

96. In our science class, we have a baro_____ so we can check the air pressure.
(A) opt
(B) meter
(C) act

---

97. Banks complete hundreds of trans_____ions each day.
(A) act
(B) miss
(C) mal

---

98. Please send your re_____tance in the form of a check or money order as soon as you get the bill.
(A) neo
(B) mit
(C) meter

---

99. The drought resulted in a crop of _____formed ears of corn.
(A) mal
(B) pan
(C) act

---

100. From the tower, we had a _____oramic view of the surrounding area.
(A) mit
(B) miss
(C) pan

INTERMEDIATE—FORM X ends on this page.

ADVANCED—FORM X
Test begins on this page.

Choose the ANTONYM for the underlined word in each sentence.

1. Researchers have deduced that the earliest dam was a stone structure built across the Nile River around 2900 B.C.

(A) concluded **(B)** classified **(C)** predicted

---

2. The Romans did not play a pivotal role in the evolution of dams.

(A) unimportant **(B)** crucial **(C)** gradual

---

3. Their main skill was the construction of aqueducts, artificial channels for transporting water.

(A) natural **(B)** unique **(C)** exemplary

---

4. During the 1930s, U.S. government agencies built many impressive dams in the United States.

(A) expensive **(B)** unremarkable **(C)** grand

---

5. Created by the order of President Herbert Hoover, the Hoover Dam is the highest concrete arch dam in the United States.

(A) destroyed **(B)** credited **(C)** designed

---

6. The Hoover Dam spans the Colorado River at the Arizona-Nevada border.

(A) crosses **(B)** avoids **(C)** splits

---

7. Lake Mead, the reservoir generated by Hoover Dam, is 115 miles long.

(A) invented **(B)** dissipated **(C)** formed

---

8. The inaccessible site chosen for Glen Canyon Dam in Arizona forced crews to drive 200 miles to cross from one side of the canyon to the other.

(A) unpredictable **(B)** remote **(C)** reachable

---

9. Initially, it took the reservoir, Lake Powell, seventeen years to completely fill with water.

(A) finally **(B)** eventually **(C)** suddenly

---

10. Since dams prohibit fish from swimming up and down a river, fish ladders allow fish to swim past the dam.

(A) prevent **(B)** allow **(C)** include

ADVANCED—FORM X

Choose the pair of words that correctly completes each analogy.

11. *Panic* is to *fear* as ______.
(A) *odd* is to *even*
(B) *nestle* is to *snuggle*

---

12. *Untidy* is to *neat* as ______.
(A) *lively* is to *listless*
(B) *polite* is to *mannerly*

---

13. *Contamination* is to *infection* as ______.
(A) *penny* is to *dollar*
(B) *overspending* is to *debt*

---

14. *Helmet* is to *armor* as ______.
(A) *moccasin* is to *slipper*
(B) *keyboard* is to *computer*

---

15. *Hoist* is to *lift* as ______.
(A) *garland* is to *wreath*
(B) *refuse* is to *agree*

---

16. *Attraction* is to *aversion* as ______.
(A) *bitter* is to *sweet*
(B) *disgrace* is to *shame*

---

17. *Blade* is to *fan* as ______.
(A) *hubcap* is to *wheel*
(B) *tool* is to *build*

---

18. *Brush* is to *paint* as ______.
(A) *mine* is to *mineral*
(B) *scalpel* is to *cut*

---

19. *Seed* is to *plant* as ______.
(A) *vacuum* is to *clean*
(B) *amicable* is to *friendly*

ADVANCED—FORM X

In each group of words below, there is a base word, two words related to the base word, and one word that is not related. Choose the word that is *not* related to the base word.

20. **(A)** unpredictable **(B)** predict **(C)** predicate **(D)** predictable

21. **(A)** venue **(B)** vent **(C)** ventilate **(D)** ventilation

22. **(A)** rigor **(B)** rigorous **(C)** rigorousness **(D)** right

23. **(A)** digest **(B)** digital **(C)** digestion **(D)** indigestion

24. **(A)** pretentious **(B)** pretend **(C)** preteen **(D)** pretense

25. **(A)** consensual **(B)** conscience **(C)** conscienceless **(D)** conscientious

26. **(A)** exception **(B)** excerpt **(C)** unexceptional **(D)** exceptionable

27. **(A)** confidence **(B)** confident **(C)** confidential **(D)** conference

28. **(A)** stately **(B)** statement **(C)** statue **(D)** statesman

29. **(A)** elevate **(B)** elementary **(C)** elemental **(D)** element

30. **(A)** personally **(B)** person **(C)** perform **(D)** personnel

31. **(A)** interrupt **(B)** interrogate **(C)** interruption **(D)** interrupted

32. **(A)** occur **(B)** occupation **(C)** occupant **(D)** reoccupy

33. **(A)** slippage **(B)** slit **(C)** slipover **(D)** slip

34. **(A)** civilian **(B)** civilization **(C)** civet **(D)** civil

Read each paragraph, and look for definition and example clues. Then use the clues to answer the questions.

Matters of etiquette, such as saying "please" and "thank you," waiting one's turn, and holding doors for others are far more than merely pleasant but inconsequential, or unimportant, behaviors. They may even be a crime-fighting tool. Odd as this may seem, it actually makes sense. This is because the central idea in etiquette involves showing respect and consideration to others. Granted, robbers, thieves, kidnappers, and other such miscreants do not commit their crimes because someone was discourteous, but many sudden and violent crimes are reactions to precisely that. Someone who is openly disrespected on the sidewalk or the highway may react with rage, and that rage can have terrible results. Can we eradicate crime—get rid of it totally—by behaving politely? Of course not, but we might reduce it. And that seems worth a try.

35. What is the definition of *etiquette?*
(A) rules that govern what is legal and illegal
(B) forms of proper or polite behavior in society; good manners

---

36. What is the definition of *inconsequential?*
(A) not meaningful or valuable
(B) not well-known; difficult to understand

---

37. What is the definition of *miscreant?*
(A) a wicked person; villain
(B) one who is guilty of a minor offense

---

38. What is the definition of *eradicate?*
(A) to remove or destroy completely
(B) to slow the growth of; to hold back

Most people today have no concept, no notion at all, about how hard it used to be to write. The act of getting one's thoughts down on paper was once a long and difficult process involving such implements as quill or fountain pens, bottles of ink, and blotters (used to soak up extra ink from the page). It is still a challenge to think of *what* to say, but a ballpoint pen and a tablet or a computer and a printer make the physical part of writing a lot easier.

39. What is the definition of *concept?*
(A) a general idea
(B) a source of information

---

40. What is the definition of *implement?*
(A) an action that serves as a step in a process
(B) something used in performing a task; tool

Colonialism in Africa

Choose the ANTONYM for the underlined word in each sentence.

41. Colonialism occurs when an outside government imposes control over the indigenous people of a faraway country.
(A) native **(C)** individual
(B) natural **(D)** foreign

42. Portuguese explorers resolutely navigated the coast of Africa during the fifteenth century.
(A) purposefully **(C)** steadily
(B) aimlessly **(D)** arbitrarily

43. Concurrently, the French and Italians began establishing new settlements in Africa.
(A) simultaneously **(C)** in cooperation
(B) soon **(D)** at different times

44. By 1884 European countries were doing their utmost to partition the country.
(A) least **(C)** odds
(B) best **(D)** maximum

45. Ethiopia, in eastern Africa, was the only African country to retain its independence during the colonial period.
(A) maintain **(C)** continue
(B) relinquish **(D)** possess

46. By 1920 a substantial portion of the African continent was under colonial rule.
(A) negligible **(C)** considerable
(B) bipartisan **(D)** terrestrial

47. Anticolonial feelings became widespread after 1950, and colonial rule began to disintegrate.
(A) unity **(C)** accord
(B) solidify **(D)** assets

48. One by one the colonies acquired their independence, and virtually all of them became independent by 1975.
(A) championed **(C)** accepted
(B) appropriated **(D)** lost

49. In Algeria, in northern Africa, the fight for independence precipitated the end of the French Fourth Republic in 1958.
(A) hastened **(C)** caused
(B) followed **(D)** delayed

50. Today it is generally believed that colonialism was an unfair and unwise disruption of the natural development of African culture.
(A) absolutely **(C)** rarely
(B) often **(D)** rightfully

ADVANCED—FORM X

Choose the pair of words that best completes each analogy.

51. *Append* is to *subtract* as ______.
(A) *adversary* is to *opposition* (B) *uncaring* is to *sympathetic*

52. *Ward* is to *hospital* as ______.
(A) *veranda* is to *house* (B) *galleon* is to *ship*

53. *Astringent* is to *constrict* as ______.
(A) *drone* is to *play* (B) *bulldozer* is to *excavate*

54. *Light* is to *brighten* as ______.
(A) *page* is to *book* (B) *vehicle* is to *transport*

55. *Register* is to *cashier* as ______.
(A) *consul* is to *embassy* (B) *megaphone* is to *announcer*

56. *Kind* is to *altruistic* as ______.
(A) *mean* is to *vicious* (B) *affectionate* is to *cold*

57. *Helmet* is to *football player* as ______.
(A) *blowtorch* is to *welder* (B) *rehearsal* is to *singer*

58. *Medicine* is to *cure* as ______.
(A) *fertilizer* is to *growth* (B) *diagnosis* is to *symptom*

59. *Dishonest* is to *treacherous* as ______.
(A) *hungry* is to *satiated* (B) *distasteful* is to *abhorrent*

60. *Calculator* is to *mathematician* as ______.
(A) *tree* is to *chainsaw* (B) *level* is to *builder*

ADVANCED—FORM X

Choose the correct definition for each underlined word.

61. We depend on American jurisprudence to maintain order and peace in our country.
(A) the police system **(B)** system or body of laws

62. An automobile accident often inhibits the flow of traffic.
(A) holds in check; restrains **(B)** redirects

63. The parents made the judicious decision to wait until their toddler was older before they bought him a dog.
(A) wise **(B)** insensitive

64. An eruption of protest followed the announcement that summer break had been cancelled.
(A) a bursting forth of something **(B)** a written complaint

65. The disruption of electrical service caused the townspeople much inconvenience.
(A) testing **(B)** breaking off of

66. One of my classmates was expelled for dying her hair green.
(A) praised **(B)** forced out

67. The artist hung his paintings on the exterior wall of his studio in hopes of selling them to the public.
(A) an outside surface **(B)** a hidden place

68. The partygoers avoided the host's best friend, who was known for his venomous attacks on people he didn't like.
(A) spiteful; full of poison **(B)** truthful

69. When the frontrunner first heard that she had been defeated, she was incredulous.
(A) unhappy **(B)** unwilling to believe

ADVANCED—FORM X

Read each paragraph, and look for comparison or contrast clues. Use those clues to answer the questions.

The Percheron is one of the largest horses in the world. Unlike a tiny Shetland pony or even a good-sized thoroughbred, a Percheron is colossal. Its size and strength made it useful in the past for pulling heavy wagons and for farm work. Today, it is coming back as a farm worker, partly due to its temperament. Although some horses can be hard to control, the Percheron is almost always docile. Tractors may be useful for many different jobs, but tractors break down. Percherons are almost as versatile as tractors but rarely break down. In addition, their four-hoof drive puts four-wheel drive to shame.

70. What is the definition of *colossal?*
(A) huge; immense
(B) able to move quickly

---

71. What is the definition of *docile?*
(A) active and energetic
(B) easily managed, trained, or taught

---

72. What is the definition of *versatile?*
(A) inexpensive to run or operate
(B) able to be used for many different functions or activities

We can now easily travel in mere days across the prairies, forests, rivers, and mountains that required months and months for early settlers to traverse. If we take to the skies, the trip can be accomplished in hours. However we travel, it is with ease and in comfort, at least in contrast to the travail of a journey by wagon train. Today, the trip is so fast that we are able to maintain our former lives unlike the settlers of the early 1800s who had to relinquish everything they had known. We, after all, can go to Colorado, Utah, Nevada, California, wherever we like, and then, whenever we like, we can return.

73. What is the definition of *traverse?*
(A) to face bravely
(B) to move across, over, or through

---

74. What is the definition of *travail?*
(A) a successful effort; accomplishment
(B) difficulty or suffering caused by hardship

---

75. What is the definition of *relinquish?*
(A) to give up completely
(B) to harm through neglect

ADVANCED—FORM X ends on this page.

TABLE OF CONTENTS
PLACEMENT TESTS FORM Y

Specific Skill Series
for Language Arts

Vocabulary

PLACEMENT TESTS

FORM Y

Primary
Intermediate
Advanced

PRIMARY—FORM Y

Test begins on this page.

Which word does *not* fit each category?

1. Things That Make Noise

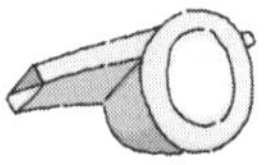

(A) whistle (B) web (C) horn

2. Things That Are Built

(A) bridge (B) house (C) knot

3. Places

(A) spray (B) store (C) school

4. Things to Wear on Your Hands

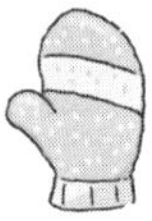

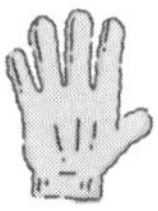

(A) mitten (B) pants (C) glove

Match each word to its synonym.

5. sick  **(A)** bake

6. cook  **(B)** weep

7. smile  **(C)** grin

8. knock  **(D)** ill

9. tall  **(E)** high

10. cry  **(F)** tap

Match each word on the left to its homograph on the right.

11. slide

(A) main stem of a tree

12. bat

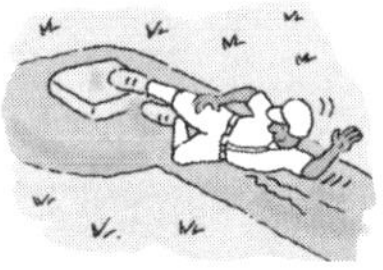

(B) to move smoothly over an area

13. ring

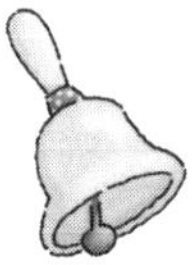

(C) a sound bells make

14. trunk

(D) a flying animal

15. saw

(E) did see

Choose a word from the box to make a compound word that describes each picture.

(A) back	**(B)** air	**(C)** yard	**(D)** pan

16. back____

17. ____plane

18. ____cake

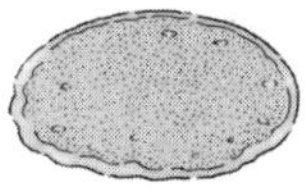

19. ____seat

What is the synonym for the underlined word in each sentence?

20. It is an <u>error</u> to write $2 + 2 = 5$.

(A) answer

(B) mistake

---

21. Can you <u>locate</u> Hong Kong on the map of Asia?

(A) change

(B) find

---

22. The trunk is usually in the <u>rear</u> of a car.

(A) inside

(B) back

---

23. The Atlantic Ocean <u>separates</u> North America and Europe.

(A) divides

(B) joins

---

24. Many cultures believe it is important to <u>honor</u> your elders.

(A) imagine

(B) respect

---

25. A snowman will <u>thaw</u> when the temperature gets warmer.

(A) fall

(B) melt

Which word pairs are antonyms?

26. (A) bold—adventurous (B) bold—shy

27. (A) agree—disagree (B) agree—over

28. (A) ancient—new (B) ancient—old

29. (A) stale—dark (B) stale—fresh

30. (A) flat—hilly (B) flat—smooth

31. (A) thick—thin (B) thick—full

32. (A) firm—tight (B) firm—loose

33. (A) soggy—soaked (B) soggy—dry

34. (A) raw—cheap (B) raw—cooked

35. (A) famous—unknown (B) famous—strange

36. (A) give—receive (B) give—gift

37. (A) present—absent (B) present—here

Choose the base word of the underlined word in each sentence.

38. The powerful jaws of a crocodile can crush the bones of large land animals.

(A) overpower

(B) power

---

39. Many products are sold in resealable bags.

(A) seal

(B) sealing

---

40. An inventor is a person who creates something new.

(A) invent

(B) reinvent

---

41. Some tortoises seem ageless because they live to be over 150 years old.

(A) aging

(B) age

---

42. Fabric that is exposed to sunlight will become discolored over time.

(A) color

(B) colored

Choose the definition of the underlined word in each context. Look for contrast clues.

43. A worker bee is <u>efficient</u>. It collects and makes honey. A drone, on the other hand, is a lazy bee.
(A) able to sleep for long hours
(B) able to do a job quickly and well

---

44. My cousin from France speaks English <u>flawlessly</u>, but I cannot speak French correctly.
(A) done without mistakes
(B) done with great speed

---

45. We expected the river's current to be moving <u>rapidly</u> because of the rain, but it had slowed down.
(A) loud
(B) fast

---

46. The coach asked the <u>entire</u> team to show up for practice, but only part of the team came.
(A) other
(B) whole

Spring

Choose the antonym for the underlined word in each sentence.

47. The coming of spring brings <u>cheer</u> to everyone.
(A) freedom **(B)** gloom **(C)** happiness

48. We <u>fill</u> our time with spring cleaning and long walks.
(A) empty **(B)** place **(C)** set

49. The softball leagues <u>begin</u> in April.
(A) go **(B)** play **(C)** finish

50. Look at those <u>bright</u> red flowers!
(A) healthy **(B)** dull **(C)** tall

51. The sky is very <u>cloudy</u> today.
(A) clear **(B)** gray **(C)** heavy

52. It is <u>wise</u> to use caution when playing outside.
(A) smell **(B)** good **(C)** foolish

53. The bird <u>builds</u> a nest to lay its eggs in.
(A) destroys **(B)** takes **(C)** makes

54. Spring may be the <u>perfect</u> season for some people.
(A) favorite **(B)** flawed **(C)** best

55. Where I live, the weather is <u>never</u> rainy during spring.
(A) almost **(B)** little **(C)** always

Read each sentence. Then choose the idiom that best matches the meaning of the underlined words.

56. The baby is grumpy and cross today.
(A) like a charm
(B) out of sorts

---

57. Don't try to avoid the issue. If you don't want to go, just tell me.
(A) beat around the bush
(B) burn the midnight oil

---

58. Before I went on stage, my acting coach told me to do a good job.
(A) chew the fat
(B) break a leg

---

59. I couldn't make up my mind, so I decided to think about it for a while.
(A) sleep on it
(B) take it easy

---

60. My shoes fit very well.
(A) fit like a glove
(B) shoot the breeze

Use the clues in each sentence to choose the prefix that belongs in the blank.

61. To arrange a party ahead of time is to ____arrange the party.
(A) re- **(B)** im- **(C)** pre-

---

62. If the computer does not work right after the first time you start it, you may have to ____start it.
(A) un- **(B)** re- **(C)** mis-

---

63. ____historic times took place before history was recorded.
(A) Im- **(B)** Bi- **(C)** Pre-

---

64. If a movie's special effects are ____realistic, they do not look real.
(A) un- **(B)** im- **(C)** re-

---

65. If you have lost something, you have probably ____placed it.
(A) pre- **(B)** mis- **(C)** im-

---

66. To pay back money that was borrowed is to ____pay it.
(A) bi- **(B)** un- **(C)** re-

---

67. If something happens that is too good to be true, it is ____believable.
(A) un- **(B)** pre- **(C)** im-

Choose the definition of the underlined word in each context. Look for contrast clues.

68. Jacob spends all his money on food and CDs. On the other hand, his sister is thrifty and would rather save her money.
(A) a big fan of music
(B) very careful with money

---

69. I expected the ocean to be calm this morning. To my surprise, the water was very choppy.
(A) rough with many waves
(B) dirty and full of seaweed

---

70. Jemal always picks up his clothes, but he only occasionally throws them in the hamper.
(A) sometimes
(B) early in the day

---

71. My neighbor's dog is obnoxious with all its late-night barking. A quiet cat would be much more likeable.
(A) unpleasant
(B) full of energy

---

72. Dad tried to resist eating the apple pie. Instead, he gave in and ate just a small bite of it.
(A) to do something quickly
(B) to try not to do something

PRIMARY—FORM Y ends on this page.

INTERMEDIATE—FORM Y

Test begins on this page.

Choose the word or words that best complete each simile or metaphor.

1. Max is as slow as a _____ in the morning because he doesn't want to go to school.
(A) glacier
(B) carrot

---

2. The noisy cicadas sound like a _____ buzzing all night.
(A) plant
(B) machine

---

3. A _____ of colorful flowers blanketed the hillside.
(A) monster
(B) rainbow

---

4. My stomach is _____ when I am really hungry.
(A) a bottomless pit
(B) a red fire engine

---

5. Our basset hound was like a _____ zooming around the backyard.
(A) race car
(B) teapot

---

6. When Paige is upset, she clenches her fists and makes her body as stiff as a _____.
(A) glass of water
(B) board

---

7. Because Jeremy hadn't studied for the oral quiz, he became a _____ when the teacher asked him a question.
(A) sponge
(B) clam

---

8. The ceiling in our classroom looks like a _____ with giant squares.
(A) checkerboard
(B) trombone

INTERMEDIATE—FORM Y

Which word pair completes each analogy?

9. *Cautious* is to *daring* as . . .
(A) *pleasure* is to *unhappiness*. **(B)** *pleasure* is to *delight*.

---

10. *Confess* is to *tell* as . . .
(A) *open* is to *close*. **(B)** *divide* is to *separate*.

---

11. *Slim* is to *slender* as . . .
(A) *near* is to *close*. **(B)** *near* is to *far*.

---

12. *Persist* is to *quit* as . . .
(A) *strength* is to *weakness*. **(B)** *frequent* is to *often*.

---

13. *Private* is to *public* as . . .
(A) *negative* is to *positive*. **(B)** *strange* is to *odd*.

---

14. *Employ* is to *hire* as . . .
(A) *salvage* is to *save*. **(B)** *salvage* is to *destroy*.

---

15. *Supplies* is to *provisions* as . . .
(A) *synthetic* is to *natural*. **(B)** *origin* is to *source*.

---

16. *Vacant* is to *full* as . . .
(A) *trustworthy* is to *reliable*. **(B)** *asleep* is to *awake*.

---

17. *Industrious* is to *lazy* as . . .
(A) *rude* is to *offensive*. **(B)** *rude* is to *polite*.

---

18. *Scorch* is to *burn* as . . .
(A) *scent* is to *odor*. **(B)** *microscopic* is to *large*.

---

19. *Major* is to *minor* as . . .
(A) *active* is to *passive*. **(B)** *persuade* is to *convince*.

---

20. *Piece* is to *portion* as . . .
(A) *outermost* is to *innermost*. **(B)** *rough* is to *uneven*.

Choose the Latin or Greek root to correctly complete each word.

21. Some fire ____ants used by firefighters can spray 1,500 gallons of water per minute.
(A) hydr
(B) ped

---

22. Sir Ernest Shackleton (1874–1922) made several ex____itions to Antarctica with the goal of reaching the south pole.
(A) ped
(B) phon

---

23. The element ____ogen was given its name because it produces water when burned.
(A) cent
(B) hydr

---

24. Singers use micro____es to transmit the sounds of their voices to large audiences.
(A) phon
(B) graph

---

25. The length of a ____imeter is 1/100th of a meter, or 0.39 inches.
(A) cent
(B) sect

---

26. When you write a research report, you should also write a biblio____y that includes the titles and authors of your sources.
(A) phon
(B) graph

Read each dictionary entry. Choose the number of the definition that fits the meaning of the underlined word in each sentence.

low (lō) *adjective.* **1.** close to the ground: *the low branches of a tree.* **2.** below what is usual or desired, as in amount, force, or degree: *low prices.* **3.** not loud; soft: *a low whisper.* **4.** depressed; gloomy: *Losing the game made him feel low.*

27. A good laugh can cheer you up when you are feeling low.
(A) 2 **(B)** 3 **(C)** 4

---

28. There was a surprisingly low voter turnout at yesterday's student council elections.
(A) 1 **(B)** 2 **(C)** 3

---

29. Frogs and toads travel by making low leaps.
(A) 1 **(B)** 3 **(C)** 4

---

ar•ti•cle (är´ ti kəl) *noun.* **1.** a piece of writing on a particular subject, forming part of a larger publication, such as a newspaper, a magazine, or an encyclopedia: *Lynn wrote an article for the school newspaper.* **2.** a particular thing or object: *Several articles were stolen from the house.* **3.** a separate clause or section of a formal document, such as a treaty, a constitution, or a contract.

30. Students were asked to bring in one article of clothing for the clothing drive.
(A) 1 **(B)** 2 **(C)** 3

---

31. Article 1 of the United States Constitution explains the powers of Congress.
(A) 1 **(B)** 2 **(C)** 3

---

32. I read an interesting article about arachnids in *Sensational Science* magazine.
(A) 1 **(B)** 2 **(C)** 3

Choose the word or words that best complete each simile or metaphor.

33. The girl in the front row was laughing like a _____.
(A) owl **(B)** rabbit **(C)** hyena

34. My uncle was as hungry as a _____ after chopping wood all morning.
(A) wolf **(B)** hummingbird **(C)** chipmunk

35. The batter ran like a _____ around the bases and slid into home.
(A) turtle **(B)** deer **(C)** elephant

36. I can't believe the _____ of homework I have left to do.
(A) pond **(B)** valley **(C)** mountain

37. Miss Thistlebottom put her finger to her lips and instructed us to be "as silent as the _____."
(A) grave **(B)** sandpaper **(C)** spinning wheel

38. The tall people standing stiffly in the photo looked like _____.
(A) cakes **(B)** telephone poles **(C)** staplers

39. The sunrise was a vibrant _____ in the dark eastern sky.
(A) hole **(B)** painting **(C)** absence

40. Lauren's hair was as silky and dark as a _____.
(A) horse's mane **(B)** soap opera **(C)** couch potato

41. The curvy road was a bright _____ in the moonlight.
(A) bowl **(B)** lightbulb **(C)** ribbon

42. Our terrier puppy was a _____ bouncing up and down.
(A) teacup **(B)** summer **(C)** spring

43. Chris said his head felt as hot as a _____ after he ate a jalapeño pepper.
(A) bucket **(B)** furnace **(C)** swimming pool

Choose the pair of words that best completes each analogy. Each analogy will compare objects to characteristics or parts to groups.

44. *Cactus* is to *prickly* as ____.
(A) *brush* is to *hair* **(B)** *python* is to *scaly*

45. *Teak* is to *wood* as ____.
(A) *pasta* is to *carbohydrates* **(B)** *freezer* is to *temperature*

46. *Corduroy* is to *fabric* as ____.
(A) *hurricane* is to *destructive* **(B)** *contract* is to *document*

47. *Diamond* is to *sparkling* as ____.
(A) *tiger* is to *fierce* **(B)** *brunch* is to *meal*

48. *Frog* is to *amphibian* as ____.
(A) *fire* is to *hot* **(B)** *minstrel* is to *musician*

49. *Cobra* is to *poisonous* as ____.
(A) *fiction* is to *literature* **(B)** *seawater* is to *salty*

50. *Scarlet* is to *color* as ____.
(A) *sand* is to *grainy* **(B)** *waltz* is to *dance*

51. *Willow* is to *tree* as ____.
(A) *problem* is to *solution* **(B)** *March* is to *month*

52. *Dollhouse* is to *miniature* as ____.
(A) *scalpel* is to *sharp* **(B)** *tin* is to *mineral*

53. *Honey* is to *sweet* as ____.
(A) *clipper* is to *fast* **(B)** *recliner* is to *chair*

Choose the Latin or Greek root to correctly complete each word.

54. Claustro_____ia is a fear of crowded or enclosed places.
(A) grat
(B) phob

---

55. A(n) _____sol can is filled with a pressurized mixture of air and another substance, such as deodorant or paint.
(A) aero
(B) grat

---

56. She is an anchor on a _____al television station that mainly reports news relating to our community.
(A) morph
(B) loc

---

57. Aqua_____ia is a fear of water.
(A) phob
(B) grat

---

58. We set the emergency brake on the car because we parked on an in_____.
(A) cline
(B) aero

---

59. The parents were _____eful to the doctor who performed successful surgery on their youngest child.
(A) loc
(B) grat

---

60. The _____space Museum in San Diego, California, features the first mailplane, called the Curtiss Jenny.
(A) Aero
(B) Phob

Read each paragraph, and look for cause-and-effect clues. Then use the clues to answer the questions.

My First Dinner Party

Because everyone was famished, they were eager for dinner. Unfortunately, I had left the roast in the oven too long, so it was burnt. The mashed potatoes were lumpy and tasted like glue. The vegetables were rubbery. A few bites of this disgusting dinner made us all feel queasy. Luckily, the ice cream I had bought was delicious!

61. What is the definition of *famished?*
(A) weak or tired
(B) very hungry; starving

---

62. What is the definition of *queasy?*
(A) sick to one's stomach
(B) having, using, or showing energy

Problem? Solution!

Marta took a tumble from her bike and got abrasions on both knees. Since she couldn't bend her legs without pain, she lurched when she walked. She looked so funny her friends couldn't help chortling. But Marta had a sense of humor. When she was ready to bike again, she joined her friends at the park with small pillows tied onto her knees, saying she'd learned not to ride without knee pads.

63. What is the definition of *abrasion?*
(A) a scraped area
(B) a brownish spot on the skin

---

64. What is the definition of *lurch?*
(A) to move in circles
(B) to move jerkily and unsteadily

---

65. What is the definition of *chortle?*
(A) to laugh softly
(B) to pay little or no attention

The Bicycle

Choose the homophone that completes each sentence.

66. The popularity of the bicycle has _____ throughout the twentieth century.
(A) grown **(B)** groan

---

67. Innovations _____ by bicycle designers in the past contributed to the development of the automobile industry.
(A) maid **(B)** made

---

68. Touring bicycles may be equipped with _____ without toe-clips to help a rider climb hills safely and efficiently.
(A) peddles **(B)** pedals

---

69. Racing bicycles are constructed using lightweight _____ alloys and other materials.
(A) mettle **(B)** metal

---

70. The _____ of the most prestigious bicycle race in the world, the Tour de France, covers about 2,000 miles.
(A) course **(B)** coarse

---

71. Winning the famous race four years in a row was quite a _____ for Lance Armstrong.
(A) feet **(B)** feat

---

72. The _____ number on a bicycle helps police to locate the owner if the bicycle is ever lost.
(A) serial **(B)** cereal

---

73. It is generally accepted that the bicycle was not invented by any _____ person.
(A) one **(B)** won

Choose the pair of words that best completes each analogy.

74. *Lobby* is to *hotel* as _____.
(A) *hurricane* is to *storm* **(B)** *banister* is to *staircase*

75. *Carburetor* is to *automobile* as _____.
(A) *nozzle* is to *hose* **(B)** *bungalow* is to *yard*

76. *Book* is to *bookcase* as _____.
(A) *plant* is to *garden* **(B)** *ceiling* is to *floor*

77. *Whistle* is to *blow* as _____.
(A) *chair* is to *sit* **(B)** *yard* is to *grass*

78. *Kitchen* is to *cook* as _____.
(A) *bark* is to *tree* **(B)** *puzzle* is to *solve*

79. *Vegetable* is to *meal* as _____.
(A) *drawer* is to *desk* **(B)** *telephone* is to *communication*

80. *Monday* is to *week* as _____.
(A) *pencil* is to *paper* **(B)** *transistor* is to *radio*

81. *Carriage* is to *ride* as _____.
(A) *butterfly* is to *flower* **(B)** *path* is to *follow*

82. *Brush* is to *paint* as _____.
(A) *radio* is to *listen* **(B)** *mountain* is to *steep*

83. *Shell* is to *nut* as _____.
(A) *day* is to *night* **(B)** *cloud* is to *sky*

84. *Needle* is to *embroider* as _____.
(A) *dirigible* is to *fly* **(B)** *frame* is to *portrait*

85. *Mouse* is to *computer* as _____.
(A) *chapter* is to *novel* **(B)** *silk* is to *satin*

86. *Garage* is to *storage* as _____.
(A) *crutch* is to *support* **(B)** *brake* is to *bike*

Use the clues in each sentence to choose the suffix that belongs in the blank.

87. A wave of immigrat______ to the United States occurred between 1870 and 1924.

(A) -ion **(B)** -ous **(C)** -ive

---

88. This wave of people was almost equivalent to four times the size of the previous group and served to further broad______ the country's diversity.

(A) -en **(B)** -ify **(C)** -ous

---

89. Many of these people were escaping poverty or religi______ persecution in their own lands.

(A) -ous **(B)** -ive **(C)** -ation

---

90. The large cities in the East were inclined to terr______ people coming from the countryside of southern and eastern Europe.

(A) -ous **(B)** -ify **(C)** -en

---

91. Many immigrants often lived together in buildings full of small, inexpens______ apartments called *tenements*.

(A) -ive **(B)** -ion **(C)** -en

---

92. Immigrants were forced to become immediately adapt______ to ways of life in the United States.

(A) -ation **(B)** -ive **(C)** -ify

---

93. These hardworking individuals would divers______ and enrich their new country.

(A) -ous **(B)** -en **(C)** -ify

---

94. Immigrants have been responsible in part for the rapid and remarkable evolut______ of the United States.

(A) -ion **(B)** -ive **(C)** -ous

Choose the Latin or Greek root to correctly complete each word.

95. Let's syn_____ize our watches to be sure we reassemble at the same time.
(A) geo
(B) chron
(C) init

---

96. Another name for *germ* is _____be.
(A) micro
(B) psych
(C) ceed

---

97. A _____osomatic illness is one for which there is no physical cause.
(A) script
(B) cede
(C) psych

---

98. A _____logist spends a lot of time studying rocks.
(A) geo
(B) chron
(C) init

---

99. The trade union decided to _____iate talks with the company's management team.
(A) micro
(B) init
(C) cess

---

100. What in_____ion did the author write in your book?
(A) psych
(B) cede
(C) script

INTERMEDIATE—FORM Y ends on this page.

ADVANCED—FORM Y
Test begins on this page.

Choose the definition for the homograph underlined in each sentence.

1. The Bayeux Tapestry is a <u>fine</u> piece of linen embroidered with scenes depicting William's victory.
   (A) of good quality **(B)** sharp

---

2. In the first scene, long before King Edward dies, he first <u>intimates</u> and then decides that William of Normandy will succeed him.
   (A) hints **(B)** close friends or associates

---

3. The tapestry describes how his advisor Harold <u>rows</u> across the English Channel to Normandy to deliver the king's message to William.
   (A) lines of people or things **(B)** uses oars to propel a boat

---

4. Harold is held hostage by a Norman <u>count</u> and then rescued by William.
   (A) say numbers in order **(B)** a nobleman

---

5. In the next scene, the tapestry <u>presents</u> the event in which Harold swears allegiance to William.
   (A) introduces **(B)** gifts

---

6. The tapestry also <u>records</u> the appearance of Halley's comet two years later in 1066 when Harold is first crowned king.
   (A) makes note of **(B)** music disks

---

7. William orders the building of a <u>fleet</u> to take him to England to seize the throne.
   (A) rapid **(B)** group of ships

---

8. The tapestry colorfully depicts the Battle of Hastings with the Norman and Saxon soldiers in a <u>grave</u> battle.
   (A) serious **(B)** place of burial

---

9. King Harald of Norway wasn't making a <u>bluff</u>, but the tapestry does not mention his invasion.
   (A) steep cliff **(B)** act of fooling

ADVANCED—FORM Y

Choose the pair of words that correctly completes each analogy.

10. *Mast* is to *schooner* as ______.
(A) *computer* is to *Web site* **(B)** *proscenium* is to *stage*

11. *Laboratory* is to *research* as ______.
(A) *cleaver* is to *cut* **(B)** *lava* is to *volcano*

12. *Penicillin* is to *cure* as ______.
(A) *lamp* is to *illuminate* **(B)** *exercise* is to *health*

13. *Propaganda* is to *persuade* as ______.
(A) *prophet* is to *follower* **(B)** *puppet* is to *entertain*

14. *Veranda* is to *house* as ______.
(A) *stamen* is to *flower* **(B)** *music* is to *listen*

15. *Riser* is to *stairs* as ______.
(A) *scuba* is to *dive* **(B)** *post* is to *fence*

16. *Molar* is to *grind* as ______.
(A) *latch* is to *fasten* **(B)** *legend* is to *map*

17. *Minaret* is to *mosque* as ______.
(A) *kindling* is to *burn* **(B)** *kickstand* is to *bicycle*

18. *Shower* is to *bathe* as ______.
(A) *enzymes* is to *digest* **(B)** *filament* is to *lightbulb*

19. *Harpoon* is to *strike* as ______.
(A) *mustang* is to *herd* **(B)** *graph* is to *measure*

20. *Morsel* is to *portion* as ______.
(A) *mandible* is to *skull* **(B)** *loom* is to *weave*

21. *Hilt* is to *sword* as ______.
(A) *eave* is to *structure* **(B)** *karate* is to *defend*

22. *Habitat* is to *biome* as ______.
(A) *hue* is to *spectrum* **(B)** *telescope* is to *view*

The United States Board on Geographic Names

Choose the base word for the underlined word in each sentence.

23. The United States Board on Geographic Names standardizes geographic name spellings for government publications.
(A) standard **(B)** stranded **(C)** standards

24. The board was originally established in 1890 by executive order of President Benjamin Harrison.
(A) oral **(B)** origin **(C)** original

25. The work of the board is the responsibility of the Secretary of the Interior.
(A) response **(B)** responsible **(C)** repose

26. The work of the board is primarily carried out by two committees.
(A) prim **(B)** primary **(C)** prime

27. The Domestic Names Committee works with state boards to standardize place-name spellings within the fifty states and United States possessions.
(A) possess **(B)** posse **(C)** possesses

28. The Foreign Names Committee relies on native maps and other material to standardize foreign geographic names for use by United States government agencies.
(A) gown **(B)** govern **(C)** governor

29. The Foreign Names Committee has developed systems for the conversion of non-Roman writing script into Roman script.
(A) convex **(B)** convert **(C)** convertible

30. Non-Roman writing scripts include Arabic and Greek, as well as the Cyrillic script which is used in Russia.
(A) write **(B)** writer **(C)** writhe

31. This ensures consistency in spellings of non-Roman names in all United States government publications.
(A) consistent **(B)** consign **(C)** consist

32. Two advisory committees composed of scientific experts help to standardize Antarctic and related terms used in oceanography.
(A) ocean **(B)** oceanic **(C)** oceanographic

Read each paragraph, and look for comparison or contrast clues. Use those clues to answer the questions.

Dogs can vary so widely that it can seem like they should be different species. Some are tiny, but others are massive. Some are friendly and easygoing; others are belligerent. One may be trusting, while another is doubtful of anyone it does not know well. Certain dogs are known for their liveliness and activity, but others are more lethargic. There are, however, certain things that are common to almost all dogs. The loyalty shown to its owner by, say, a German shepherd is much the same as the fidelity of any other dog.

33. What is the definition of *massive?*
(A) costly or expensive
(B) having great size and weight

---

34. What is the definition of *belligerent?*
(A) eager to fight
(B) warmly affectionate

---

35. What is the definition of *lethargic?*
(A) easily frightened; timid
(B) showing little strength, energy, or alertness

---

36. What is the definition of *fidelity?*
(A) continuing faithfulness
(B) the condition of being dependent

Burkina Faso and Ghana are neighboring countries in western Africa. Burkina Faso's economy is predominantly agricultural, and Ghana's is also based mainly on farming. Ghana has access to the Atlantic Ocean, which forms its southern border, but Burkina Faso is landlocked. Whereas Ghana is rich in mineral resources, Burkina Faso is almost devoid of them. Both nations are poor by world standards, but Ghana's economy is healthier than that of Burkina Faso.

37. What is the definition of *predominantly?*
(A) for the most part; chiefly
(B) in a way that is impractical

---

38. What is the definition of *landlocked?*
(A) surrounded by land
(B) unable to be reached by land

---

39. What is the definition of *devoid?*
(A) well-supplied
(B) entirely without; lacking

Astronomy

Choose the word that best completes the metaphor in each sentence.

40. The stars in the constellations of the night sky are connect-the-______ drawings on an infinite black sheet of paper.
(A) doughnuts **(B)** dot **(C)** doorknobs

---

41. Earth is a blue and white ______ as seen from space.
(A) marble **(B)** wave **(C)** wrinkle

---

42. The sun was a huge orange ______ slowly sinking into the ocean.
(A) star **(B)** statue **(C)** ball

---

43. In ancient times, people said our galaxy was a river of white ______ in the sky.
(A) bubbles **(B)** ice **(C)** milk

---

44. Jupiter is the ______ of planets; more than 1,300 Earths could fit inside of it.
(A) prince **(B)** king **(C)** president

---

45. Binary, or double stars, are ______ twirling around one another at a ball.
(A) dancers **(B)** yarn **(C)** narcissists

---

46. The eyes of Danish astronomer Tycho Brahe were ______ that earned him recognition as one of the greatest early astronomers.
(A) galaxies **(B)** telescopes **(C)** stickers

---

47. Strangely enough, Brahe's nose was the ______ that attracted much of the attention, not his astronomical achievements.
(A) city **(B)** community **(C)** magnet

---

48. Brahe lost his nose in a duel and was forced to wear a fake one made of gold; it was a bright, shining ______, like the one that he loved to study.
(A) furnace **(B)** sun **(C)** flashlight

ADVANCED—FORM Y

Choose the pair of words that best completes each analogy.

49. *Stair* is to *escalator* as ______.
(A) *cockpit* is to *airplane* **(B)** *helicopter* is to *propeller*

50. *Tan* is to *sunburn* as ______.
(A) *gemstone* is to *mine* **(B)** *singe* is to *scorch*

51. *Tranquilize* is to *perturb* as ______.
(A) *emancipate* is to *enslave* **(B)** *dilapidate* is to *crumble*

52. *Cajole* is to *wheedle* as ______.
(A) *evade* is to *pursue* **(B)** *harass* is to *irritate*

53. *Tine* is to *fork* as ______.
(A) *follicle* is to *hair* **(B)** *pick* is to *guitar*

54. *Pleased* is to *exultant* as ______.
(A) *lie* is to *steal* **(B)** *giggle* is to *chortle*

55. *Paint* is to *illustrator* as ______.
(A) *instructor* is to *classroom* **(B)** *squeegee* is to *window washer*

56. *Airplane* is to *travel* as ______.
(A) *suitcase* is to *transport* **(B)** *ambulance* is to *siren*

57. *Weaken* is to *debilitate* as ______.
(A) *hunger* is to *famine* **(B)** *hysterical* is to *amusing*

58. *Cornea* is to *eyeball* as ______.
(A) *building* is to *cornerstone* **(B)** *course* is to *curriculum*

59. *Embody* is to *personify* as ______.
(A) *embellish* is to *adorn* **(B)** *embrace* is to *shun*

Choose the correct definition for each underlined word.

60. New York City is a great fashion metropolis.
(A) city regarded as the center of something
(B) type of stage

---

61. Advertisers sometimes view cities with certain characteristics as microcosms of the larger United States.
(A) contradictions
(B) miniature representation of a large whole

---

62. The doctor told the diabetes patient to eat dietetic sweets and to limit sugar intake in general.
(A) prepared for use in special diets
(B) low in calories

---

63. The author's latest book is more exoteric than her earlier work.
(A) lacking in quality or depth
(B) belonging to the outer circle or more general population

---

64. After undergoing three rounds of chemotherapy and radiation treatments, the cancer was in remission, and the patient's prognosis was good.
(A) mood; attitude
(B) prediction of the outcome of a disease

---

65. In one Olympic summer sport, swimmers synchronize their movements while in the water.
(A) make to happen at the same time
(B) listen to

---

66. The apathetic babysitter talked on the phone and did her nails while the baby cried in her crib.
(A) indifferent; lacking emotion
(B) lacking skills

---

67. It is rare that a person's face or body is completely symmetrical.
(A) balanced in proportions
(B) rounded

---

68. During the heated debate, each candidate accused the other of being a demagogue.
(A) hypocrite
(B) unprincipled leader of the people

Read each paragraph, and look for cause-and-effect or general context clues. Then use those clues to answer the questions.

To get an idea of what it was like to be a soldier at Valley Forge, spend the winter there. Wrap your body in only a thin blanket and your feet in rags so the cold permeates every part of you. Sleep, when you can, in a rough hut. When you are so hungry that you feel you might succumb to starvation if you don't eat, have a thin pancake. Spend your days training. Do all this, and you will have a sense of what the soldiers in George Washington's Continental Army endured.

69. What is the definition of *permeate?*
(A) to spread throughout
(B) to become aware of; to notice

---

70. What is the definition of *succumb?*
(A) to resist
(B) to give in; to yield

Even if you could duplicate the physical conditions with which soldiers had to cope at Valley Forge, you could not duplicate those soldiers' emotional conditions. They had to watch nearly a quarter of their comrades die from disease. They had to worry about whether their families could survive without them, about the skirmishes and more major battles to be faced in the spring, and about whether they would ever get paid. And, while they froze and starved, they had to think about how the British were living in warm houses in Philadelphia. Because the British were being invigorated by regular hot meals and sound sleep, they were probably in better shape. Perhaps most importantly, they didn't know what you know—that their side in this brutal war would eventually prevail. They did what they did, suffered what they suffered, with hope alone to keep them going.

71. What is the definition of *cope?*
(A) to deal with
(B) to become aware

---

72. What is the definition of *skirmish?*
(A) a training exercise
(B) a brief or minor conflict

---

73. What is the definition of *invigorate?*
(A) to challenge
(B) to fill with strength and energy

---

74. What is the definition of *prevail?*
(A) to be victorious; to triumph
(B) to look into the future; to predict

ADVANCED—FORM Y ends on this page.

Name ______________________________ Date ____________

Form: ❑ X ❑ Y Test Level: ❑ Primary ❑ Intermediate ❑ Advanced

❑ Grammar	❑ Usage	❑ Mechanics
❑ Spelling	❑ Vocabulary	❑ Sentences
❑ Paragraphs	❑ Writing Process	❑ Research

1. ______	23. ______	45. ______	67. ______	89. ______	111. ______
2. ______	24. ______	46. ______	68. ______	90. ______	112. ______
3. ______	25. ______	47. ______	69. ______	91. ______	113. ______
4. ______	26. ______	48. ______	70. ______	92. ______	114. ______
5. ______	27. ______	49. ______	71. ______	93. ______	115. ______
6. ______	28. ______	50. ______	72. ______	94. ______	116. ______
7. ______	29. ______	51. ______	73. ______	95. ______	117. ______
8. ______	30. ______	52. ______	74. ______	96. ______	118. ______
9. ______	31. ______	53. ______	75. ______	97. ______	119. ______
10. ______	32. ______	54. ______	76. ______	98. ______	120. ______
11. ______	33. ______	55. ______	77. ______	99. ______	121. ______
12. ______	34. ______	56. ______	78. ______	100. ______	122. ______
13. ______	35. ______	57. ______	79. ______	101. ______	123. ______
14. ______	36. ______	58. ______	80. ______	102. ______	124. ______
15. ______	37. ______	59. ______	81. ______	103. ______	125. ______
16. ______	38. ______	60. ______	82. ______	104. ______	126. ______
17. ______	39. ______	61. ______	83. ______	105. ______	127. ______
18. ______	40. ______	62. ______	84. ______	106. ______	128. ______
19. ______	41. ______	63. ______	85. ______	107. ______	129. ______
20. ______	42. ______	64. ______	86. ______	108. ______	130. ______
21. ______	43. ______	65. ______	87. ______	109. ______	
22. ______	44. ______	66. ______	88. ______	110. ______	